M000012044

# HELLO
## SONshine

DEVOTIONAL

Forty Days of Encouragement
and Journaling for Women

Heather Petty

TRILOGY CHRISTIAN PUBLISHERS
*TUSTIN, CA*

Trilogy Christian Publishers
A Wholly Owned Subsidiary of Trinity Broadcasting Network
2442 Michelle Drive
Tustin, CA 92780

Manufactured in the United States of America

10 9 8 7 6 5 4 3 2 1

Library of Congress Cataloging-in-Publication Data is available.

ISBN 978-1-64773-650-7

ISBN 978-1-64773-651-4 (ebook)

# Contents

# Dedication

To

Riley Jason,

stillborn,

08/09/1995

# Acknowledgements

A very special thank you to:

Our Lord and Savior, who has so beautifully pieced my life together in such a way that He could speak life, love, hope, and grace to me and through me. There will never be enough words to describe my humble gratitude for His presence in my life.

My husband, Mitch, who has always encouraged me and never stopped believing in me, even when I did not (or could not) believe in myself. He is one of the kindest, most gentle souls I know – always behind the scenes, never taking any recognition, and leading our family with humility, grace and love

My precious twin sister, Heidi. Having the privilege of doing life with a twin is literally having the perfect friend. I wish you could meet her – she is beautiful inside and out, has the kindest, most giving heart, and is truly a reflection of Jesus. I could write about her for days and still not begin to glorify the courageous, strong, and gracious woman she is.

My sweet daughter, Emily – my "angel baby" for her heart for Jesus, her heart to serve, and her ability to give both amazing grace and a tiny bit of truth. When I first sent examples of my writing to my editor, I commented, "What if she isn't touched by them?" Without hesitation, Emily said, "I don't know how that is even possible; God has given you a gift." Very humbling.

My mom and grandma, who both showed me unconditional love, kindness, and instilled in me a heart to serve those less fortunate, to love the unlovely, and to give without limits. They, too, survived a harsh world and persevered with courage and the utmost strength.

My niece, Katie, my daughter, Baileigh, and my dear friend and sister in Christ, Janet, who have all shared in the vision of Love and SONshine Ministries. And to my two sons, Jake and Parker – both of whom have such incredible hearts for the Lord. Their faith often inspires me and has given me great encouragement over the years. All of these people have loved me through so many seasons of life – the messy, the beautiful, the times of deep grief and sorrow, and everything in between.

To my precious fellowship ladies – Michele, Toni, Jennifer, Annie, and Deena – who have seen both the beauty and the ugly in my life, yet loved me without judgment. Even in my darkest times, when I felt like I had failed as a wife, mother, friend, and a Christian – they were there, always holding me up, praying for me, and reminding me of the enemy's "big, fat lies!" These ladies are my sisters in Christ, and the love I have for them can't be measured.

To Jeremy and Kaci Neely, Alison Carson, and Loulita Gill, all of whom gave encouragement, displayed God's love, and helped bring this devotional together. These individuals were brought into my life only by God's hand. They are some of the most beautiful Christians I have had the pleasure to know and work with.

**And to all of YOU, I am forever grateful and so blessed by your presence in my life. Love you!**

# Welcome and Encouragement from Heather

Hello, beautiful SONshine! I am so glad you are here with me. Know that the Lord Himself knew you would be here reading this devotional at this very moment. Why? Because He chose you long before you were ever in your mother's womb. In fact, each day we meet through this devotional, it is a divine appointment, ordained especially by the Lord. And know that, beyond a shadow of a doubt, He is here, right now, walking with you in this very moment. No matter what you may be facing, your Savior is here. Feel Him, embrace Him, and allow Him to transform your life over the next forty days. Welcome to our SONshine family – a family where Jesus (the SON of man) is a reflection of the very core of our being.

This devotion is dedicated to my eldest son, Riley, who was born sleeping. At the time, I did not know how I would go on or whether I would ever feel whole again. After Riley, my husband and I had two more children: Emily, who I call my "angel baby" because I feel that having her actually saved my life, and Jake, who I now endearingly call "Jakerz" (mainly because he wouldn't appreciate still being called Jakey!).

Throughout my younger years, I experienced so much heartache and pain that led me to feel extremely inadequate. My entire being was riddled with guilt and shame. As a result of my brokenness, I looked to anything and anyone for approval, and I lived for many years inside the shell of a human, where I hid everything just to survive. Then, after the loss of Riley and the births of Emily and Jake, sadly, through a course of events, my marriage ended in divorce.

As only the Lord could do, He brought a wonderful man into my life who would love my two precious kids and me. I also gained my eldest daughter, Baileigh, who is such a joy. She is gentle, kind, and passionate about life. Together, my second husband and I walked through several miscarriages and finally had our amazing son, Parker. Parker was born with his own health issues that saw him undergo his first surgery at just three months. Parker has the biggest heart and has never let his health get in the way of being the young man he is today.

After seven years into my second marriage, I finally told my husband all about my life – the secrets, the shame, and the deep pain I had buried deep inside for so many years. And guess what? He loved me anyway, just like Jesus did. NO ... MATTER ... WHAT!

Despite all the challenges I have encountered in life, I have often felt God's presence, especially in the dark times. About eighteen years ago, I finally surrendered my life entirely to the Lord. That is when this journey began. I am SO thankful you are all here with me to share in the grace, joy, and redemption of knowing our precious Jesus.

The Lord has reminded me repeatedly of just how much He loves me, and He loves each one of you equally as much! As I prayed about what to write, the Lord brought me to the parable of the lost sheep:

> Then Jesus told them this parable: "Suppose one of you has a hundred sheep and loses one of them. Doesn't he leave the ninety-nine in the open country and go after the lost sheep until he finds it? And when he finds it, he joyfully puts it on his shoulders and goes home. Then he calls his friends and neighbors together and says, 'Rejoice with me; I have found my lost sheep.' I tell you that in the same way there will be more rejoicing in heaven over one sinner who repents than over ninety-nine righteous persons who do not need to repent" (Luke 15:3-7).

In this story, the good shepherd (God) leaves ninety-nine sheep to go and search for the one who was lost.

Why would God leave the ninety-nine to search for just one? Here is why – because of His love. 1 John 4:8 beautifully and simply states the revelation of God's nature in just three words: *God is love.* God is love, and He will never, ever stop loving you. Your identity is that of a daughter of God, regardless of the choices you've made, the things you have or have not done, or what others think of you.

In joining me on this forty-day journey, I pray that you will find joy, and most of all, that you will feel loved unconditionally as the beautiful and treasured woman you are. You, my dear sister, are the daughter of the Most High, Jesus Christ. And to Him, there is NONE more precious. So, straighten your crown and take your royal position as a daughter of the King of kings!

## About Love and
## SONshine Ministries

I'd like to tell you a little bit about the history of Love and SONshine Ministries.

Two scriptures have been instrumental in the term 'SONshine' – which, to me, means YOU (yes, you) are a reflection of Jesus, the SON of God.

*The SON is the radiance of God's glory...* Hebrews 1:3.

I also love The Message version: This SON perfectly mirrors God, and is stamped with God's nature. He holds everything together by what he says – powerful words.

*"So if the SON sets you free, you will be free indeed."* John 8:36.

Here's how it all began: My daughter, Emily, was going through a very difficult season at high school, and so, I started sending her daily text messages beginning with the words, "Hi, SONshine!" The messages contained relevant encouraging scriptures for her to receive during schooltime. Sometimes, I would also write the verse Matthew 19:26 on her arm in the mornings (*"With man*

*this is impossible, but with God all things are possible"*).
Gradually, my other children and some of their friends
asked to receive these text messages, and it developed
into a group of about sixty youngsters. This small group
was a safe place to share my thoughts, my writing, my
heart, and most importantly, our Jesus.

Though many people asked and encouraged me to
put these messages into a book, I was terrified! I felt
inadequate.

Three years ago, I developed the courage to take the
ministry to social media, and now here you are reading
this devotional! All because God took a very unequipped
person (me) and gave me a new heart (*"I will give you
a new heart and put a new spirit in you; I will remove from
you your heart of stone and give you a heart of flesh"* Ezekiel
36:26).

My hope is that this devotional will bring you both love
and SONshine. I am so excited to walk this journey
with you.

# Using This Devotional

Why forty days of SONshines? I chose forty for two reasons:

1.  God placed it on my heart.

2.  Because the number forty often shows up in Scripture. For me, the two most significant '40s' are connected with our Lord Himself:

    *   Jesus was tempted after fasting for forty days and nights (Matthew 4:1-11). Jesus was not tempted when He was surrounded by friends or family; He was tempted when He was alone, hungry, and vulnerable. This shows us that He was one hundred percent human and can identify with us on every level.

    *   There were forty days between Jesus' resurrection and ascension (Acts 1:3). In those forty days, Jesus appeared to the women at the tomb, to His disciples, and to many other people, showing us with certainty that He was and is the Messiah. He later gave His disciples the Great Commission: *"All authority in heaven and earth has been given to me. Therefore go and make disciples of all nations..."* and then He fin-

*ished by saying, "And surely I am with you always, to the very end of the age"* (Matthew 28:18-20).

Through this devotional, you, too, can discover the significance of these '40s' – that God knows you, loves you, and is always with you.

Each devotion contains:

- a short reading
- a corresponding scripture for you to meditate on
- one or more question to ponder
- a place to journal your thoughts

Find a space that works for you and a time that will fit with your schedule, but don't feel pressured that it must be the same every day. The important thing is to invite the Lord to be with you. Ask Him to pull up a chair and join you. Feel His presence and allow Him to speak directly to your heart.

Know that I, along with a few others, have prayed for each of you and will continue to pray for you. We love you, sweet sister!

# 1 The Tiny Church

Hello, *SONshine!*

I have to tell you a story of something incredible that happened a few years ago. I met a wonderful Christian man named Martin, and I told him that my son was attending college in his hometown.

Being the kind man that he is, Martin reached out to my son and took him (and a few others) in. He and his wife, Darla, treated them like their own. They had them over to their house, cooked them dinner, and prayed for them.

My husband and I have been so grateful for them – we've always prayed for other adults to come into our children's lives and influence them for Christ.

Fast forward several months, we went to our son's college to watch his team play football. While there, Martin invited us to his church.

It was a sweet little church, absolutely filled with the Holy Spirit. We walked in, and I immediately got goosebumps. Everything – from the music and the sermon, to Mary, the sweet lady who sat next to me – moved me. It was something I had been longing for – that spark, that tingle in my tummy, that joy – for a while!

Sitting in that church, worshiping with all those people, the Spirit stirred in me to be bold in my faith. A little intimidated, and feeling very inadequate, I took a step and started the Love and SONshine Ministries Facebook page.

See, I believe that meeting Martin and Darla was far more for ME and YOU than it was for my son. It was a 'divine' appointment that only God, in His mighty power, could have orchestrated.

For those of you who don't know me, the Lord has placed it on my heart to share with others my story, my joy, and all that the Lord has done for me. The Facebook page was the start of that, and now this devotional is another part of it.

## Scripture

*being confident of this, that he who began a good work in you will carry it on to completion until the day of Christ Jesus*

**Philippians 1:6**

## Questions to ponder

What is your story?

Is God asking you to boldly step out in faith and share it?

# Journal

........................................................................

........................................................................

........................................................................

........................................................................

........................................................................

........................................................................

........................................................................

........................................................................

........................................................................

........................................................................

........................................................................

........................................................................

........................................................................

........................................................................

........................................................................

# 𝟚 The Hard Shell

Hello, *SONshine!*

While helping a friend with some landscaping, I had the task of shoveling a mound of dirt and hauling it to another location. The outside of the pile had hard snow on it and was difficult to break through. But once I got that top layer off, the dirt became softer and much easier to shovel.

It made me realize that my life had been much like that pile of dirt. For many, many years, I was just a (VERY) hard shell on the outside. Deep down, there was always a softness, but it took many years for me to let myself be vulnerable enough for anyone to see that.

You see, I endured so much over the years that I had completely closed myself off to others. There was only one, maybe two, who really knew me. Ultimately, as a result of my hardened outside, I ended up even more wounded.

Thankfully, I found the Lord – or rather, HE FOUND ME. He had been pursuing me for numerous years, but I kept running away. After all, if anyone knew my heart, they would know too much. Did I really think that God didn't already know it all?

I'll never forget that moment of surrender. Tears streamed down my face, and I felt a tingling sensation in my stomach. I knew, without a doubt, that I could no longer ignore God's pursuit. For the first time in my life, I felt forgiven ... and loved. Truly loved! Since that time, God has pieced my life back together so perfectly in the way that only our Creator could do.

Sweet lady, redemption is for anyone. When our Jesus went to the cross, it was for you, precious girl. You are His daughter, His princess, His love. There is nothing you can do (past, present, or future) to make Him love you any less than He does right at this very moment. What a beautiful gift!

My prayer for everyone is that they find and know this great freedom. Have you accepted Jesus as your Lord and Savior? If you haven't, would you like to? Feel free to use the prayer at the back of this book.

## Scripture

*This is good, and pleases God our Savior, who wants ALL people to be saved and to come to a knowledge of the truth*

**1 Timothy 2:3-4**

## Question to ponder

Are there any 'hard' areas in your life that have been caused by pain and suffering?

Allow God's love to saturate your soul today and begin softening that outer layer.

# Journal

........................................................
........................................................
........................................................
........................................................
........................................................
........................................................
........................................................
........................................................
........................................................
........................................................
........................................................
........................................................
........................................................
........................................................
........................................................

# 3 Becoming Fearless

Hello, SONshine!

There is often so much uncertainty in our lives and, as a result, it is easy to become fearful. Fear can be crippling to the point of affecting our physical, emotional, and spiritual health. Throughout the Bible, "Fear not" or "Do not be afraid" are used hundreds of times.

One time in my life when I really battled with fear was when I was pregnant with my youngest son, Parker. I made it through the first twenty weeks without having a miscarriage, so I thought I was 'home free'. But at my mid-way ultrasound, the technician found that he had a congenital birth defect, one that would require multiple surgeries. In addition, this particular defect is often accompanied by one of two types of chromosome abnormalities – one would leave him developmentally disabled, and the other would have the added consequence that he would pass away shortly after birth. I was not angry with God, but I was definitely afraid.

Trusting God and relying on Him completely is our greatest weapon against fear. And the good news is that

He is one hundred percent trustworthy for His character, and His nature never changes! Throughout Scripture, not only does God constantly reminds us not to fear, but He also reminds us of the very important fact that He is with us. God's words and promise in Isaiah 41:10 tells us: *"So do not fear, for I am with you; do not be dismayed, for I am your God. I will strengthen you and help you; I will uphold you with my righteous right hand."*

Regardless of what we may be facing, God is still (and will ALWAYS be) in control. My sweet Parker is now 16. God is good! Love you!

## Scripture

*When I am afraid, I put my trust in you*

**Psalm 56:3**

## Questions to ponder

What are you most afraid of right now?

What aspect of God's character and nature do you need to trust to overcome your fear?

# Journal

...........................................................

...........................................................

...........................................................

...........................................................

...........................................................

...........................................................

...........................................................

...........................................................

...........................................................

...........................................................

...........................................................

...........................................................

...........................................................

...........................................................

# 4 A Grateful Heart

Hello, *SONshine!*

After my grandma passed away, I wondered what the holidays would be like without her. Her birthday was in late November so, each year on Thanksgiving, our entire family would get together and celebrate her birthday. I wish each of you could have had the opportunity to meet her – she smiled with her eyes, and I always felt like I could see right down into her soul.

Do you know what I saw in her soul? Unconditional love, grace, compassion, mercy, and warmth. She would joke that she "raised a hundred kids," and I reckon that wasn't too far from the truth. Everyone was welcome at her table.

As I reflected on what holidays without Grandma would be like, I remembered a song I listened to growing up. It's called "Jesus, I Heard You Had a Big House," and one line says, *"Jesus, I heard about meal time, when all Your children come to eat."* I smiled, thinking of Grandma and her large table, not to mention her large heart, especially for those less fortunate.

Her generosity came out of a heart of gratitude.I think that is exactly how the Lord wants our tables (and our hearts, homes, the things we have, etc.) to be available for others. I am so very grateful for the many lessons I learned from my grandma, but most of all, the legacy of giving she left in the hearts of so many.

## Scripture

*The generous will themselves be blessed,*
*for they share their food with the poor*

**Proverbs 22:9**

## Question to ponder

Do you find it difficult to give
without limits?

Consider why that might be. Cultivate
gratitude by thinking about what you have
instead of what you want.

# Journal

..........................................................................
..........................................................................
..........................................................................
..........................................................................
..........................................................................
..........................................................................
..........................................................................
..........................................................................
..........................................................................
..........................................................................
..........................................................................
..........................................................................
..........................................................................
..........................................................................
..........................................................................

# 5 Chosen

Hello, *SONShine!*

Have you ever felt like you just don't fit in? I can recall situations from my childhood that made me feel this way – like when I didn't get picked for the 'good' sports team, when I wasn't part of the 'popular' crowd, and when I couldn't participate in something because I wasn't part of a particular community or even church.

Throughout the gospels, we see that Jesus was 'all-inclusive' – anyone was welcome at the table of the Lord. The story of Levi, the tax collector, comes to mind.

At that time, tax collectors were hated. Yet, Jesus personally called Levi, and Levi followed Him. When the Pharisees saw Jesus eating at Levi's house, not only with Levi but with other tax collectors and sinners as well, they questioned His disciples about it, saying, *"Why does he eat with tax collectors and sinners?"* To which Jesus replied, *"It is not the healthy who need a doctor, but the sick. I have not come to call the righteous, but sinners"* (Mark 2:16-17).

Friends, even as Christians, we can sometimes feel like we don't belong, but the truth is that we have been adopted into the family of God, and we do belong (see John 1:12-13 and Ephesians 1:5)!

If, for any reason, you feel like you don't belong, come to the Lord's table. Jesus welcomes all. You don't have to be part of a certain group, you don't have to be popular, and you don't have to be picked for a team. Because, to Him, we are all invited – all we have to do is accept His invitation.

Love you!

# Scripture

*Let anyone who is thirsty come to me and drink. Whoever believes in me, as Scripture has said, rivers of living water will flow from within them." By this he meant the Spirit, whom those who believed in him were later to receive*

**John 7:37-39**

# Questions to ponder

Think about a time when you felt like you didn't fit in. How did it make you feel?

How can you use this to learn to be all-inclusive?

# Journal

.....................................................................
.....................................................................
.....................................................................
.....................................................................
.....................................................................
.....................................................................
.....................................................................
.....................................................................
.....................................................................
.....................................................................
.....................................................................
.....................................................................
.....................................................................
.....................................................................
.....................................................................

# 6 Rest in Jesus

Hello, *SONshine!*

As a full-time working mother, my days off typically start with a lengthy to-do list. I don't often get days to myself so that I can accomplish the extra things that need to be done. One specific time when I had a day off, I already had a whole list of things I needed (wanted) to do. But, at the end of a very busy work week, I was exhausted – to the point that I spent almost the entire day in bed!

Later that day, as I thought about everything I hadn't achieved, the Lord brought one word to my mind: Peace! So often, we hear the phrase "rest in peace" when someone passes away, yet we don't LIVE in peace. I wonder how and why our lives get so busy!

If your family is like ours, you'll know what it's like to feel that the days and nights sometimes seem like a whirlwind – even a blur. But that's not how the Lord intended us to live. There are many scriptures about peace. One of my favorites is John 14:27, which records these precious words of Jesus: *"Peace I leave with you; my peace I give you. I do not give to you as the world gives. Do not let your hearts be troubled and do not be afraid."*

Friends, if you're exhausted – maybe you work too much and/or spend all your efforts trying to be a good wife, mom, and friend – take a step back and rest. Rest in the peace that only Jesus can give.

Sometimes, taking a break is what we need most. Although I didn't accomplish anything on my to-do list that day, I think I accomplished exactly what Jesus wanted me to – to rest, to regroup, and to be human. And, most importantly, to turn my focus back to Him.

## Scripture

---

*"Come to me, all you who are weary and burdened, and I will give you rest. Take my yoke upon you and learn from me, for I am gentle and humble in heart, and you will find rest for your souls"*

**Matthew 11:28-29**

## Question to ponder

---

Is there an area in your life where you need rest (serving others, housework, social media, etc.)?

# Journal

........................................................................

........................................................................

........................................................................

........................................................................

........................................................................

........................................................................

........................................................................

........................................................................

........................................................................

........................................................................

........................................................................

........................................................................

........................................................................

........................................................................

........................................................................

# 7 Healing

Hello, SONShine!

Many of you may not know that, for many years, I battled with a distorted body image and the constant desire to be thin. I was a compulsive exerciser – at times, I would exercise for several hours and drink only water.

In addition, I relied on those around me to meet my emotional needs, because I constantly craved approval. As a result, I worked myself to exhaustion, struggled with depression, made choices I regretted, and never felt like I would measure up. Out of this unhealthy self-view grew anger, resentment, and many unmet expectations.

During one of the darkest times in my battle, I started sobbing – you know, the snot-bubble sob. I couldn't take these burdens anymore. I cried out to Jesus! I remember my words exactly: "Just take it from me! I don't want this anymore! Just take it!"

While I knew I still had a long road ahead of me to 'undo' all that had been done over the years, I emphatically knew I was not alone. I could feel the comfort, love, and supernatural peace of the Holy Spirit.

Often, when we cry out in prayer, we want healing (or whatever it is) to happen right that instant. God can do that, but many times, He uses these things for our growth and for His purpose (not ours). Jeremiah 29:11 says, *"For I know the plans I have for you," declares the Lord, "plans to prosper you and not to harm you, plans to give you hope and a future."*

Sweet sister, rest in the knowledge that God is alive and at work in our lives. Whatever it is in your life that needs healing (external or internal), give it to God. Whether He heals you immediately or not, be assured that His grace is enough. No matter what, He can be trusted, and He is always with you. Love you!

# Scripture

*Surely he took up our pain and bore our suffering, yet we considered him punished by God, stricken by him, and afflicted. But he was pierced for our transgressions, he was crushed for our iniquities; the punishment that brought us peace was on him, and by his wounds we are healed. We all, like sheep, have gone astray, each of us has turned to our own way; and the Lord has laid on him the iniquity of us all*

**Isaiah 53:4-6**

# Question to ponder

Is there an area in your life that needs healing?

Ask God for help, believe that He IS at work in you and trust Him with the end result.

# Journal

..................................................................

..................................................................

..................................................................

..................................................................

..................................................................

..................................................................

..................................................................

..................................................................

..................................................................

..................................................................

..................................................................

..................................................................

..................................................................

..................................................................

..................................................................

# 𝓢 A Father's Love

Hello, *SONShine!*

Our youngest son had been trying to save money for an item he wanted. My husband and I gave him a few extra jobs to do around the house to help him earn money. One of his jobs was to clean all of the windows – inside and out. When it came time for him to clean the higher outside windows, I noticed my husband on the ladder, cleaning them for him.

I thought, "Boy, that's a good deal! Dad does your job, and you get paid. I want that job!" When I joked with my husband about it, he said, "I'm not putting him on this ladder. It's not very sturdy, and I don't want him to fall." At that moment, my heart filled with so much love and gratitude. I felt like I was looking straight into the eyes of Jesus – I could see the love a father has for his child. He would put himself in harm's way to protect his child from getting hurt.

This is exactly what Jesus did for us when He willingly went to the cross to pay for our sin. Not His sin, because Jesus was without sin, but OUR sin. When I read through Scripture, particularly the gospels, I often find myself asking the question, "Why me?" Why would Jesus do this for ME when I've fallen short so many times, over and over again? And every time I've asked that question, I've heard Jesus reply, "Because you are My child."

Not every one of us has an earthly father who displays the love of Jesus. In fact, many have 'daddy issues' as I've heard it termed. But know that the only perfect father is God – look to Him for how a daddy should be. The human in us finds it difficult to comprehend the love our heavenly Father has lavished on us, but I saw a perfect example of it in my husband's love for our son that day.

## Scriptures

*Let grace, mercy, and peace be with us in truth and love FROM God the Father and from Jesus Christ, Son of the Father!*

**2 John 1:3, MSG**

*See what great love the Father has lavished on us, that we should be called children of God! And that is what we are!*

**1 John 3:1**

## Question to ponder

How has your earthly father shaped you?

Now allow your heavenly Father to shape you and your beliefs about His love.

# Journal

..........................................................................

..........................................................................

..........................................................................

..........................................................................

..........................................................................

..........................................................................

..........................................................................

..........................................................................

..........................................................................

..........................................................................

..........................................................................

..........................................................................

..........................................................................

..........................................................................

..........................................................................

# 9 The Other Side of Death

Hello, SONshine!

I had the great joy (yes, joy) of attending a funeral. It was for someone I had never met, the sister of a dear friend. This young woman had passed away after an almost two-year battle with cancer. She was young, leaving behind her husband, teenage daughter, and SO many friends and family members.

Though I did not personally know this beautiful woman, hearing about her made me feel like she was an old friend, someone with whom I could just pick up where we left off each time we met. I felt like her heart was exactly like the heart I want to have – a heart for Jesus and a heart for others.

Though her physical loss was mourned, there was also joy and rejoicing in knowing the place to which she had gone. Heaven! Most of us have heard the descriptions of heaven – that its streets are paved with gold, its walls and foundations made of precious gems, and its gates made of pearls (Revelation 21:18-21). I believe those things to be literally true, but I also believe heaven is so much more than our human minds can ever think or imagine. No more suffering, no more tears, no more pain; absolutely complete in Christ.

And just as it was so eloquently spoken at the funeral, this young lady's sole goal in life was to live totally surrendered to Jesus and His will, even if His will was her earthly death. Friends, that is faith. We do not know what this side of life holds for us, but one thing we can be assured of is what the other side of death holds. Either eternity with Him or without Him. And we get to choose!

## Scripture

---

*For to me, to live is Christ and to die is gain*

**Philippians 1:21**

## Question to ponder

---

In what ways do you feel led to surrender
your life to God's will?

# Journal

....................................................................

....................................................................

....................................................................

....................................................................

....................................................................

....................................................................

....................................................................

....................................................................

....................................................................

....................................................................

....................................................................

....................................................................

....................................................................

....................................................................

....................................................................

....................................................................

# 10 The Cardboard Sign

*Written by Heidi Williams (my sweet twin)*

Hello, SONshine!

Several years ago, I was driving home from work after a long, exhausting day. I was also hungry and thirsty, so I went through a drive-through and bought something to eat so that I didn't have to prepare anything when I got home. As I pulled up to a stoplight, I noticed an unkempt old man with long, dirty hair and missing teeth. He was a regular there and carried the usual sign 'Vietnam Vet, anything helps, God bless.' As I made eye contact and smiled, the Lord whispered, "He's hungry, too." I thought to myself, "Oh, Lord, please not tonight. I'm so tired and weary." But the Lord persisted.

You see, God calls us to feed and clothe the poor, to serve them as though we are serving Christ. When I approached him, I reached out my hand to grab his and noticed that he was filthy, his nose was dripping, and he smelled bad. Much to my surprise, he was wearing a portable catheter. We made small talk as I gave him my food. He told me his name and that he had a trailer. His arthritis was acting up badly that day, he said, so he was having a hard time walking anywhere to get food.

As I drove away, I wondered what Jesus really looks like. The Bible says that He was not a handsome man, and He knew sadness (Isaiah 53:2-8); He had few material possessions (Luke 9:58); He was laughed at and scorned (Matthew 9:24); His own brothers rejected Him (John 7:5); He knew hunger (Matthew 4:2); He wept (John 11:35); And He endured the greatest of human sufferings (Isaiah 50:6, Isaiah 52:14; Matthew 27:26).

I never saw that man again, and I often pass that street corner and wonder, "Was he an angel placed there to strengthen my walk with God?"

## Scripture

*Do not neglect to show hospitality to strangers, for thereby some have entertained angels unawares*

**Hebrews 13:2**

## Questions to ponder

What does Jesus look like in your life?

Is He just a mere afterthought when things aren't going right, or when you are stressed out?

Do you call upon His name in every circumstance of your life?

What does your giving look like?

Are you willing to love like Jesus?

# Journal

..........................................................................

..........................................................................

..........................................................................

..........................................................................

..........................................................................

..........................................................................

..........................................................................

..........................................................................

..........................................................................

..........................................................................

..........................................................................

..........................................................................

..........................................................................

..........................................................................

..........................................................................

# 11 You Are Not Alone

Hello, *SONshine!*

Have you ever noticed that social media is a highlight reel of people's lives? Very rarely do we see the raw, inner person displayed on these platforms. Instead, we see beautiful family pictures, proud mom and dad moments, and beautifully edited selfies.

But not everything in life is as perfect as social media might lead us to believe. I think we all wrestle with internal battles, many of which no other person will ever know about. On the outside, it can appear that some people have a perfect life and the perfect family. If we're not careful, we can judge our lives against this false image, leaving us feeling broken and alone.

Have you ever experienced the overwhelming feeling that you will never be as perfect as everyone else? I've been there, standing in the midst of those very emotions. Sometimes, it feels like a tornado is swirling around you, like the world is closing in.

When this happens, cry out to Jesus. He will give you His supernatural peace. The tornado may not always stop swirling, but His peace will cover you. I love the beautiful words in a song by Casting Crowns that states, "Oh, my soul, you are not alone." There are no truer words.

# Scriptures

*And the peace of God, which transcends all understanding, will guard your hearts and your minds in Christ Jesus*

**Philippians: 4:7**

*"And I will ask the Father, and he will give you another advocate to help you and be with you forever – the Spirit of truth. The world cannot accept him, because it neither sees him nor knows him. But you know him, for he lives with you and will be in you. I will not leave you as orphans; I will come to you"*

**John 14:16-18**

# Question to ponder

In your life, in what ways have you felt inadequate?

Ask God to reveal His truths to you and to give you peace.

# Journal

....................................................
....................................................
....................................................
....................................................
....................................................
....................................................
....................................................
....................................................
....................................................
....................................................
....................................................
....................................................
....................................................
....................................................
....................................................

# 12 Agape Love

Hello, *SONshine*!

I have a picture I once took of my feet in the clear, blue waters of Glacier National Park! Looking at it, I was reminded of the meaning behind the tattoo on my foot that says the word 'agape'.

Agape love is **selfless, sacrificial, and unconditional love.** It is the highest of the four types of love mentioned in the New Testament and is the love Jesus shows us. Agape love, however, is also the way we should love God. Jesus said it perfectly: *"You shall love the Lord your God with all your heart, with all your soul, with all your strength, and with all your mind,' and 'your neighbor as yourself"* (Luke 10:27).

See, agape love is different from human love – agape is loving the unlovely and the unlovable! Whether others are fellow believers or not, we are called to love with agape love. This type of love does not come naturally and is not based on a feeling or emotion. It is a deliberate, willful act to choose to see the best in people, to hold them in the highest regard. You can only understand

and give this type of love when you understand the love your heavenly Father has for you. At times, when I have struggled to demonstrate agape love, I have said to myself, "That person is God's child, too."

My twinnie always says, "Love them to the Kingdom," which is exactly what we do when we love with agape love!

# Scripture

*"Greater love has no one than this: to lay down one's life for one's friends"*

**John 15:13**

# Questions to ponder

Have you ever known someone who was simply unlovable?

Do you think God placed them in your life for a reason?

Sometimes, God places people on our paths to teach us how to love with agape love – will you pass the test?

# Journal

........................................................................

........................................................................

........................................................................

........................................................................

........................................................................

........................................................................

........................................................................

........................................................................

........................................................................

........................................................................

........................................................................

........................................................................

........................................................................

........................................................................

........................................................................

# 13 Forgiveness

Hello, SONshine!

One of my favorite Bible verses (I know I always say "it's one my favorites"!) is found in Matthew. It's a verse that talks about forgiveness. Some of you may know that my Instagram and Twitter accounts are 'CrazyChristian77'. The '77' part is from Matthew 18:22 which emphasizes forgiving over and over again, *"not seven times, but seventy-seven times."*

At the time of Jesus, the rabbis (the Jewish teachers) taught people to forgive, but only three times. Peter, then, was probably feeling quite generous when he asked Jesus if seven times was enough. Jesus' answer, *"I tell you, not seven times, but seventy-seven times,"* tells us that we should not pay attention to a number, but forgive people as often as is necessary.

To some, forgiveness seems like a weakness! In reality, forgiveness requires great strength! It has nothing to do with whether or not the offending person deserves it; it is a deliberate act of love, mercy, and grace – the very thing the Lord extended to us! God's salvation in Christ is the ultimate example of forgiveness!

Let me encourage you to forgive others and accept God's forgiveness for your own sins! IT WILL SET YOU FREE!

## Scriptures

*If we confess our sins, he is faithful and just and will forgive us our sins and purify us from all unrighteousness*

**1 John 1:9**

*Bear with each other and forgive one another if any of you has a grievance against someone. Forgive as the Lord forgave you*

**Colossians 3:13**

## Questions to ponder

Is there a person you need to forgive (even if it is yourself)?

# Journal

# 14 A Masterpiece

Hello, *SONshine!*

While reading Rick Warren's book The Purpose Driven Life, I came across this powerful statement: *"Anytime you reject any part of yourself, you are rejecting God's wisdom and sovereignty in creating you."*

God delights in you! Every little detail about you is a masterpiece designed by your Creator. In Genesis 1:26-27, we are told that we are made in the image of God. The culture we live in is always screaming, "You are not good enough. If only you were thinner, if only you were younger, if only you could fit into those jeans you wore in high school." If only, if only, if only (blah, blah, blah).

The truth is God does not make ANY mistakes. He made us to be a reflection of His glory. We have the ability to reflect His character of love, grace, mercy, patience, compassion, forgiveness, and faithfulness.

Go and look in the mirror and choose to love everything about yourself – from your physical appearance to all the beautiful qualities God has given you.

# Scriptures

*For we are God's masterpiece. He has created us anew in Christ Jesus, so we can do the good things he planned for us long ago*

**Ephesians 2:10, NLT**

*For you created my inmost being; you knit me together in my mother's womb. I praise you because I am fearfully and wonderfully made; your works are wonderful, I know that full well. My frame was not hidden from you when I was made in the secret place, when I was woven together in the depths of the earth. Your eyes saw my unformed body; all the days ordained for me were written in your book before one of them came to be*

**Psalm 139:13-16**

# Questions to ponder

What do you love about yourself?

How can you focus on being made in God's image?

# Journal

....................................................................

....................................................................

....................................................................

....................................................................

....................................................................

....................................................................

....................................................................

....................................................................

....................................................................

....................................................................

....................................................................

....................................................................

....................................................................

....................................................................

....................................................................

# 15 Grandma's Prayer

Hello, SONshine!

I was blessed to have my grandma in my life for almost fifty years. Some of my sweetest memories of our time together are from when I used to bathe her. She was one of the greatest spiritual influences in my life. She passed away when she was a few months shy of turning 100 years old; her mind was slowly fading, and she often couldn't remember "which one I was" (I am an identical twin). Her hearing and eyesight had also faded, so it was sometimes difficult for her to follow a conversation.

Yet, the one thing that never wavered through the years was her faithfulness to prayer. Whenever I arrived at her home, and whenever I left, she would hold me in her arms and say, "God bless you, walk with you, and keep you." An immediate peace would pour over me, and I would remember that I was not alone.

I often reflect on my life's journey and wonder how many of my family members prayed for me, even those who lived before I was born and never knew me personally. Friends, there is a battle over our families today; the enemy would love nothing more than to destroy anything dear to us, especially our kids. Prayer for our children and families is essential in order for us to stay alert and discern the voice of God.

Remember: Prayer + God's Word = Power!

# Scripture

*The Lord bless you and keep you; the Lord make his face shine on you and be gracious to you; the Lord turn his face toward you and give you peace*

**Numbers 6:24-26**

# Question to ponder

Think of a person who has influenced your walk with Christ and write a prayer thanking the Lord for them. Friend, if you can't think of a person, know that I have personally prayed for you many times. You are not alone with Jesus by your side.

Which family members can you pray for right now?

Commit to praying for them regularly.

# Journal

..................................................
..................................................
..................................................
..................................................
..................................................
..................................................
..................................................
..................................................
..................................................
..................................................
..................................................
..................................................
..................................................
..................................................
..................................................

# 16 New Life

Hello, SONshine!

Recently, new life has been on my mind. Memories of our dogs when they were pups have popped up on my Facebook timeline. And news of sweet mama's having babies seems to be all around.

No matter what country you live in, new life (babies of any kind – human or animal) has been statistically shown to bring joy. Have you ever watched an elderly person holding a baby? I think of my mom and grandma – I can't even describe their joy, their smile, and their love for babies.

All of us experienced 'new life' when we were brought into this world. But there is another kind of 'new life' that we have the opportunity to experience as well. It's new life in Christ when we accept Jesus as our Lord and Savior. In 2 Corinthians 5:17-18, the apostle Paul wrote: *Therefore, if anyone is in Christ, the new creation has come: The old has gone, the new is here! All this is from God, who reconciled us to himself through Christ and gave us the ministry of reconciliation.*

When an addition to my church was being built, all the members were able to write a verse on the unfinished floors and walls. That is the verse I wrote. At the time, I was fairly new in my walk with the Lord – but I knew one thing! I had been made new – no more guilt, shame, fear, worry, people-pleasing, or the like, for me. Do you know how freeing that was and still is?

Friends, as a believer in Jesus Christ, you have new life! Lay all your burdens at the cross. Celebrate the joy of the greatest gift you have been given – both NEW LIFE and ETERNAL LIFE!!

## Scripture

---

*Praise be to the God and Father of our
Lord Jesus Christ! In his great mercy he
has given us new birth into a living hope
through the resurrection of Jesus Christ
from the dead, and into an inheritance
that can never perish, spoil or fade*

**1 Peter 1:3-4**

## Question to ponder

---

Did you know that accepting Jesus as your
Lord and Savior made you a new creation
of great worth?

You are made entirely new. The old has
gone, the new has come!

# Journal

..................................................
..................................................
..................................................
..................................................
..................................................
..................................................
..................................................
..................................................
..................................................
..................................................
..................................................
..................................................
..................................................
..................................................
..................................................
..................................................

# 17 A Lasting Legacy

Hello, SONshine!

Throughout my career, I've often been in leadership roles where I was responsible for making hiring decisions, and I have acquired a handful of 'favorite' questions to ask interviewees. One of these questions is: "At the end of your career (or life), what will your legacy be?" This is usually followed up with the related question, "What will people say about you?"

While I know what type of answers I am looking for, I've often thought about these questions for my own life. Very humbling to think about, right? What will people say about me when I'm gone? What will my legacy be? As these questions have surfaced in my mind recently, I've realized that I honestly don't care if anyone remembers anything about me except that Jesus lived in me and that I was His hands and feet.

Over the years, I told my children many times, "You may be the only Bible a person ever reads." As I opened my Bible and asked the Lord for direction in writing this devotion, He brought me to 2 Corinthians 3:2-3: *You yourselves are our letter, written on our hearts, known and read by everyone. You show that you are a letter from Christ, the result of our ministry, written not with ink but with the Spirit of the living God, not on tablets of stone but on tablets of human hearts.*

Friends, don't let the world around you make you numb. Keep believing in the good, keep showing kindness, and keep leaving the legacy of Christ's love. Eternity is at stake.

# Scripture

*You did not choose me, but I chose you and appointed you so that you might go and bear fruit – fruit that will last – and so that whatever you ask in my name the Father will give you. This is my command: Love each other*

**John 15:16-17**

# Questions to ponder

What will your legacy be?

At the end of your life, what will your friends and family have to say about you?

# Journal

....................................................................

....................................................................

....................................................................

....................................................................

....................................................................

....................................................................

....................................................................

....................................................................

....................................................................

....................................................................

....................................................................

....................................................................

....................................................................

....................................................................

....................................................................

....................................................................

# 18 Religion vs. Faith: What's the Difference

Hello, SONShine!

My sweet twinnie has a very good explanation of the difference between religion and faith: Religion typically asks you to try to reach God by DOING something (saying certain prayers, wearing certain clothing, avoiding certain foods/beverages, observing certain 'holy' days, etc.). Whereas faith ... faith is allowing God to reach you!

Being in a works-based religion only leads to feelings of inadequacy and insecurity. Why? Because you are always trying to do more, be better, stop certain things, etc. But faith believes that God has already done everything necessary for us to be made right with Him. In fact, before salvation, our 'works' were done in the flesh and could not please God; even our most 'righteous' deeds fell far short of God's glory (see Isaiah 64:6 and Romans 3:20).

Does this mean there is no place for religion? Not necessarily. But what the Bible tells us about religion is best summed up in James 1:27 – *Religion that God our Father accepts as pure and faultless is this: to look after the orphans and widows in their distress and to keep oneself from being polluted by the world.*

While many religions care for others and do good works, none but Christianity offers salvation by grace through faith (Ephesians 2:8-9). It is only through a personal relationship with Christ that salvation is achieved. This allows the Holy Spirit to dwell within you, and as a result, you will increasingly want to care for and love others (do good works). Not because you MUST – but because you WANT to (as a result of God moving in your heart).

Good works should always be motivated by faith and only to glorify God!

# Scripture

---

*You are the light of the world. A town built on a hill cannot be hidden. Neither do people light a lamp and put it under a bowl. Instead they put it on its stand, and it gives light to everyone in the house. In the same way, let your light shine before others, that they may see your good deeds and glorify your Father in heaven*

**Matthew 5:14-16**

# Questions to ponder

---

In what ways has your heart changed towards others since being saved?

How can this be demonstrated through good works to the glory of God?

# Journal

...................................................................

...................................................................

...................................................................

...................................................................

...................................................................

...................................................................

...................................................................

...................................................................

...................................................................

...................................................................

...................................................................

...................................................................

...................................................................

...................................................................

...................................................................

# 19 The Scapegoat

Hello, SONshine!

The resurrection of Jesus changed all the rules. See, before Jesus' sacrificial death and glorious resurrection, people had to bring sin offerings (animals) to the Lord as an atoning sacrifice for their sins.

Have you ever heard of the term 'scapegoat'? In Leviticus chapter 16, it speaks of two goats – one was to be offered to the Lord as a sacrifice, and the other was to be a scapegoat. The first goat represented the forgiveness of sin, and the second represented the removal of sin.

The scapegoat was sent to a remote place, escorted by an appointed person, where it was released. The goat, God said, would *carry on itself all their sins* (Leviticus 16:22).

Can you imagine that little goat looking back at its keeper, wondering why he had to be sent away? Maybe the goat hesitated as he was told, "Go on," and chased into the wilderness to carry the people's sins away for good.

The Day of Atonement, on which these events happened, was Israel's most solemn day. On this day of the year, God made a way for sinful people (all of us) to get right with Him. This old system of sacrifice was temporary and had to be repeated every year. The new system of sacrifice, Jesus' death on the cross, is permanent.

The scapegoat was a foreshadowing of Jesus' death on the cross, the atonement for all of our sins once and for all. See, God knew that nothing in our humanness could atone for our sins. So, He sent His one and only Son to be the final scapegoat for everyone. That, my friends, is LOVE!

# Scripture

*Unlike the other high priests, he [Jesus] does not need to offer sacrifices day after day, first for his own sins, and then for the sins of the people. He sacrificed for their sins once for all when he offered himself*

**Hebrews 7:27**

# Something to Think About

Holding on to sin is saying the cross was not enough. It can be very hard to let go of past sin, guilt, and shame, but it's important to let it go.

# Questions to ponder

Is there something you need to let go of?

Ask the Holy Spirit to help you release whatever it is. Write a prayer of thanksgiving and rejoice in this freedom.

# Journal

........................................................

........................................................

........................................................

........................................................

........................................................

........................................................

........................................................

........................................................

........................................................

........................................................

........................................................

........................................................

........................................................

........................................................

........................................................

# 20 Faithful Obedience

*Written by Emily Johnson (my sweet daughter)*

Hello, SONShine!

I often find myself doubting God, thinking, "God, can You really make this happen? Will You really ALWAYS provide?" And every single time, God prevails.

However, it's very difficult in our humanness to put our entire faith and trust in God because we want to do everything ourselves. I know I always think, "If I don't do it, it'll never get done!" Thankfully, that's not how God works. He calls us to trust Him and let Him work out the details according to HIS plan.

We see this unfold in the account of Ruth the Moabite, one of the most loyal women in history. When Ruth lost her husband, she lost the source of her stability and safety. But instead of remaining in her own country and seeking to remarry, she chose to leave everything behind to take care of her mother-in-law, Naomi, who had decided to return to Israel.

After arriving in Israel, Ruth set out to find leftover grain so that she and Naomi could eat. She happened to gather barley in the field of Boaz, a wealthy Israelite who was also a kinsman-redeemer in Naomi's family. Eventually, Boaz married Ruth, which secured the future of both Ruth and Naomi.

I love this story, because it shows that obedience and loyalty can lead us right to where we are supposed to be, even if it is hard to see at the time. Ruth had no idea that her loyalty would lead her to a better life, but God knew – *and* His plans included her being in the lineage of the Messiah! When we fully trust God and obey Him, He will lead us to a life filled with His blessings.

## Scripture

*But Ruth replied, "Don't urge me to leave you or to turn back from you. Where you go I will go, and where you stay I will stay. Your people will be my people and your God my God"*

**Ruth 1:16**

## Question to ponder

Is there an area of your life in which God is asking you to trust and obey Him?

# Journal

....................................................
....................................................
....................................................
....................................................
....................................................
....................................................
....................................................
....................................................
....................................................
....................................................
....................................................
....................................................
....................................................
....................................................
....................................................

# 21 Fully Trusting God

Hello, SONshine!

I stumbled upon a verse one time that really stuck with me: *Those who trust in their riches will fall, but the righteous will thrive like the green leaf* (Proverbs 11:28).

So often, we place our trust in material things such as financial security, a good job, or having a nice home or car. Yet, none of these things are permanent. The two things that everyone has in common are life and death. At the end of our lives, no one will remember all the 'things' we had during our lifetime. Therefore, material things do *not* define us. Our identity can only be found in Christ.

Do you remember the rich man who asked Jesus, *"What must I do to inherit eternal life?"* (Mark 10:17, NLT)? Though the rich man had kept God's commandments, Jesus knew what was holding him back. Looking at the man, Jesus felt genuine love for him. *"There is still one thing you haven't done,"* he told him. *"Go and sell all your possessions and give the money to the poor, and you will have treasure in heaven. Then come, follow me"* (verse 21).

The rich man's response revealed that he was not prepared to trust Jesus more than his own wealth: *At this the man's face fell, and he went away sad, for he had many possessions* (verse 22). His trust lay in the temporary things of the earth; Jesus wanted him to trust Him, where true riches are found.

# Scripture

"Do not store up for yourselves treasures on earth, where moths and vermin destroy, and where thieves break in and steal. But store up for yourselves treasures in heaven, where moths and vermin do not destroy, and where thieves do not break in and steal. For where your treasure is, there your heart will be also"

**Matthew 6:19-21**

# Questions to ponder

Sister, what is it you're holding on to?

What is keeping you from living God's best life?

Pray and ask Him to reveal to you what He is calling you to do. Just maybe, it is to sell everything and devote your life to service

(I know there is someone who needs to hear this today).

# Journal

..................................................................

..................................................................

..................................................................

..................................................................

..................................................................

..................................................................

..................................................................

..................................................................

..................................................................

..................................................................

..................................................................

..................................................................

..................................................................

..................................................................

..................................................................

# 22 Valuable You

Hello, SONshine!

While studying the life of Jesus in the book of Luke, I started to see more of Jesus' character. He didn't seek to gain approval from others; rather, He sought the lost – the sinner, the broken, the hurting, and the poor.

There are many stories of Jesus and His servant's heart, but one of the most powerful is the account of when He washed His disciples' feet. You see, this menial task was usually reserved for the lowest slave. In washing their feet, Jesus reminded His disciples that they were to serve one another and not expect to be served.

Jesus is the ultimate example of a servant. Laying down His life by dying on a cross for our sins was the greatest demonstration of servanthood. It was a high price to pay so that you and I could have eternal life.

Where were you when Jesus found you? In a bar? At the gym? At college? At church? Wherever you were, Jesus (the SAVIOR) came looking for you! Why? Because YOU are valuable to Him. You are worth every single moment of the search. And when you answered His call to surrender – ALL the angels rejoiced over you (Luke 15:10). And NOW – YOU are His beloved child, one of His chosen people, a royal priesthood, a holy nation (1 Peter 2:9).

I hope by reading about the life of Jesus, you can see and learn just how valuable YOU are to Him. Love you so much!

# Scripture

*He laid aside his outer garments, and taking a towel, tied it around his waist. Then he poured water into a basin and began to wash the disciples' feet and to wipe them with the towel that was wrapped around him*

**John 13:4-5, ESV**

# Thought for Today

If I asked you to think of all the things you love (or cherish, adore, or find beauty in) – how long would it take you to think of yourself?

# Questions to ponder

If I asked you to think of all the things you love (or cherish, adore, or find beauty in)

In what ways has it been difficult for you to see yourself through the eyes of Christ – as His valuable daughter? How has today's devotion helped to shape your understanding of your value and identity in Christ?

# Journal

........................................................

........................................................

........................................................

........................................................

........................................................

........................................................

........................................................

........................................................

........................................................

........................................................

........................................................

........................................................

........................................................

........................................................

........................................................

# 23 God's Grace

Hello, SONshine!

Throughout my life, I've thought so much about grace. Sometimes, just thinking about it makes me choke up. This FREE gift is given to us through our faith in Jesus Christ! He knows our every secret, every mistake, every shortcoming, and yet, still loves us unconditionally and gives us His grace – freely.

Many people believe that salvation through grace is a complex process that happens over a lifetime of doing good works. Living in the bondage of a works-based thought process will only leave you desperate for hope, feeling like you will never measure up – lost, lonely, broken, alone, and searching for something (or someone) you will never find. See "things" (works, deeds, searching for significance) will always come to an end. Having a personal relationship with Jesus Christ will never end – it is infinite.

Grace is often most needed and best understood in the midst of pain, brokenness, and sin. Grace is God's favor toward the unworthy. In His grace, God is willing to forgive us and love us unreservedly, even though we don't deserve it. We live in a world of earning, deserving, and merits (works) – all of these only lead to judgment. Judgment kills, whereas grace makes us alive!

Without God's grace, we would be hopelessly lost. Instead, we are saved (by His grace and not by our own works).

## Scriptures

*For it is by grace you have been saved, through faith – and this is not from yourselves, it is the gift of God – not by works, so that no one can boast*

**Ephesians 2:8-9**

*This righteousness is given through faith in Jesus Christ to all who believe. There is no difference between Jew and Gentile, for all have sinned and fall short of the glory of God, and all are justified freely by his grace through the redemption that came by Christ Jesus*

**Romans 3:22-24**

## Question to ponder

Sweet SONshine – do you, like me, sometimes wonder how a God so powerful, so mighty, so perfect could love you, a sinner with so many 'black marks' on your life slate?

Because YOU are His precious child, and to Him, there is none more precious! Love you!

# Journal

.........................................................................

.........................................................................

.........................................................................

.........................................................................

.........................................................................

.........................................................................

.........................................................................

.........................................................................

.........................................................................

.........................................................................

.........................................................................

.........................................................................

.........................................................................

.........................................................................

.........................................................................

# 24 My Best Friend

Hello, SONshine!

Wikipedia defines friendship as *"a relationship of mutual affection between people. It is a stronger form of interpersonal bond than an association."*

Throughout the Bible, there are verses about friendship. For example, Proverbs 27:9 (MSG) says that *a sweet friendship refreshes the soul.* See, Jesus knows our desire to love and be loved. Our friends can be our greatest source of joy, love, encouragement, wisdom, kindness, empathy, honesty, forgiveness, understanding, and compassion.

Having a true friend is one of our greatest treasures, for they are people who allow us to be ourselves without judgment. I have a few very beautiful friends like this. Sometimes, I am a total space – that is, I get lost in my own world, but one of my friends once told me, "I love you for your spaciness!" A true friend sees your flaws and loves you anyway!

Jesus desires this type of friendship with you – a strong, intimate connection. And He wants you to be real, not hiding behind only the good things in your life. He wants you to be honest with Him – He already knows anyway! He understands your human limitations, and He loves you for who you are. Whether you are spacy like me, or you have your own imperfections, Jesus loves you! As Proverbs 17:17 says: *A friend loves at all times.*

# Scriptures

A sweet friendship refreshes the soul

**Proverbs 27:9, MSG**

"No longer do I call you servants, for the servant does not know what his master is doing; but I have called you friends, for all that I have heard from my Father I have made known to you"

**John 15:15**

And the Scripture was fulfilled that says, "Abraham believed God, and it was counted to him as righteousness" – and he was called a friend of God

**James 2:23**

# Question to ponder

What can you do today to nurture your friendship with Jesus?

# Journal

........................................................
........................................................
........................................................
........................................................
........................................................
........................................................
........................................................
........................................................
........................................................
........................................................
........................................................
........................................................
........................................................
........................................................
........................................................
........................................................

# 25 Well Done

Hello, SONshine!

My hubby and I went for a fairly long walk one evening. After a long day, I knew I was close to reaching my 10,000-step goal, but my Fitbit watch didn't start buzzing. When I looked at it after our walk, my watch said I had walked close to 12,000 steps. It turned out that I had accidentally turned off the notifications. I was so bummed – I wanted the recognition that I had met my goal for that day.

I thought about this and our lives. You hear of all kinds of recognition programs at schools and workplaces, and every year, all the people in Hollywood wait in anticipation to see if they've been nominated for some big award.

One of our most inherent desires is to be noticed for our hard work. In Luke 19:11-27, Jesus told a parable about three servants whose master gave them each 10 minas (a certain amount of money). The first doubled the money he was given. The second earned five additional minas, but the third buried the money and only gave back to his master what he had been given in the first place. To the first servant, the master said, *"Well done, my good servant! Because you have been trustworthy in a very small matter, take charge of ten cities."* Similarly, the second servant was put in charge of five cities. The final servant, however, was called wicked, and all of his minas were taken away from him and given to the first servant.

This parable shows us two different attitudes toward Jesus – one that diligently prepares for His return, and one that is complacent, without a heart for doing the work of the kingdom.

I've shared this story because the greatest recognition we can ever receive is to be told by our Creator, "Well done, good and faithful servant!" There is NO earthly recognition that will ever compare to hearing those words. It is our ultimate goal!

## Scripture

"His master replied, 'Well done, good and faithful servant! You have been faithful with a few things; I will put you in charge of many things. Come and share your master's happiness!'"

**Matthew 25:21**

## Question to ponder

Where or from whom do you seek recognition?

How can you use your time, talents, and treasures to serve God's kingdom?

# Journal

....................................................................
....................................................................
....................................................................
....................................................................
....................................................................
....................................................................
....................................................................
....................................................................
....................................................................
....................................................................
....................................................................
....................................................................
....................................................................
....................................................................
....................................................................

# 26 A Safe Place

Hello, SONshine!

Here is another story about my sweet grandma.

Once, when visiting her near to the end of her earthly life, I arrived to find that she was in bed (she had been bedridden for some time). She appeared to be sleeping, so I put my hand on her shoulder and whispered, "I'm here, Grandma. It's Heather." Immediately, she grabbed my hand and asked me to stay with her. As I sat down next to her, as I used to as a little girl, all I could think of was 'safety'.

Grandma and Papa's house was always a safe place! No matter what fears I had or what was going on around me, it was always a safe place. There, I was free of all worry and fear, and I knew that no 'booger man' could get me. It was, indeed, a safe place, a place of pure peace.

I'm sure that's what Jesus wants us to know about His presence – that it's a safe place. He is the place where we can be our true selves with nothing hidden – just the real, the raw, the people we are. There's no guilt, shame, fear, or worry in His presence. He is our place of safety and peace.

Friends, if you are feeling fearful, anxious, depressed, guilty, or worried, go to that place. Go to Jesus! Your feelings may not go away entirely, but I guarantee that you will feel safe.

# Scriptures

*In peace I will lie down and sleep, for you alone, Lord, make me dwell in safety*

**Psalm 4:8**

*The Lord is my light and my salvation – whom shall I fear? The Lord is the stronghold of my life – of whom shall I be afraid?*

**Psalm 27:1**

*Whoever dwells in the shelter of the Most High will rest in the shadow of the Almighty. I will say of the Lord, "He is my refuge and my fortress, my God, in whom I trust"*

**Psalm 91:1-2**

# Questions to ponder

Where do you feel safe?

How can you rest in the safety of God's arms today?

# Journal

..................................................................
..................................................................
..................................................................
..................................................................
..................................................................
..................................................................
..................................................................
..................................................................
..................................................................
..................................................................
..................................................................
..................................................................
..................................................................
..................................................................
..................................................................

# 27 Sweet Fayisa (Son Koo)

Hello, *SONshine!*

With permission, I want to tell you of an incredible young man whom God so beautifully placed in my life. When I first met him, I did not fully understand his culture nor the basic needs of the people in his Ethiopian village – food, clothing, clean water, and shelter. His father left when he was five, so it is just him and his mom.

As he and I have become closer (in fact, he now calls me "Mom Koo" – 'koo' means 'mine'), my heart hurts because I wish I could give him and his mom the kind of life people enjoy here in the United States.

In praying for him, the Lord brought me to Matthew 25:31-46, where Jesus spoke about the final judgment. Verse 40 impacted me the most: *"Truly I tell you, whatever you did for one of the least of these brothers and sisters of mine, you did for me.'"*

See, we show our belief and faith in God by how we act and how we give. Every day, we can be generous in our actions. For example, by offering encouragement, praying for others, showing kindness and compassion, and giving of ourselves (emotionally or financially).

Wonderful Son Koo once wrote this to me: "When you give me something ... I said to myself, 'How is it done to me? Why she give me like this? Why she doesn't refuse/ignore me?' I get this all question only for one answer – it is God's work."

Many of us have been so richly blessed and yet want to hold on to things as if they belong to us. But the reality is that everything we have belongs to God. Friends, if you have someone on your heart who may need your time, talents, love, or even a financial gift – GIVE. In doing so, you are giving directly to our sweet Jesus!

## Scripture

❋

*"'For I was hungry and you gave me something to eat, I was thirsty and you gave me something to drink, I was a stranger and you invited me in, I needed clothes and you clothed me, I was sick and you looked after me, I was in prison and you came to visit me'"*

**Matthew 25:35-36**

## Question to ponder

Is there a person on your heart to serve in some way?

Ask God to give you direction, and know that no matter how big or small, Jesus sees.

# Journal

....................................................................

....................................................................

....................................................................

....................................................................

....................................................................

....................................................................

....................................................................

....................................................................

....................................................................

....................................................................

....................................................................

....................................................................

....................................................................

....................................................................

....................................................................

....................................................................

# 28 A Broken Heart

Hello, SONshine!

I remember a time my heart broke! It broke for someone I had been fervently praying for. She made a decision that day that would change her life forever. It was the one thing I had prayed so diligently she wouldn't do – yet, things were just too overwhelming, and she did it anyway.

I found myself deeply saddened for her. While I know her decision wasn't my fault, I still somehow felt responsible. Maybe if I'd prayed harder, maybe if I'd said more or done more ... maybe, maybe, maybe.

In fact, I was so upset that I needed to talk to someone. I tried to call people close to me, but no one answered. After a few tries, I heard the words, "Call Me!" And then I heard it again, "CALL ME!" Call Jesus! His heart was breaking too; I could literally feel Him crying with me.

I won't ever understand some things, but I know for certain that I am never alone, the person I had prayed for is never alone, and YOU are never alone. When you're struggling like I was, call Jesus! He will ALWAYS pick up when you call! Love you!

# Scriptures

The Lord is close to the brokenhearted; he rescues those whose spirits are crushed

**Psalm 34:18, NLT**

"'Call to me and I will answer you and tell you great and unsearchable things you do not know'"

**Jeremiah 33:3**

# Question to ponder

Think about a time when your heart broke and you could do nothing about it. How did you handle it?

How will knowing that God is always with you and always waiting for you to turn to Him change the way you may handle heartache in the future?

# Journal

.......................................................
.......................................................
.......................................................
.......................................................
.......................................................
.......................................................
.......................................................
.......................................................
.......................................................
.......................................................
.......................................................
.......................................................
.......................................................
.......................................................
.......................................................

# 29 Comfort

Hello, *SONshine!*

2 Corinthians 1:3-4 says: *Praise be to the God and Father of our Lord Jesus Christ, the Father of compassion and the God of all comfort, who comforts us in all our troubles, so that we can comfort those in any trouble with the comfort we ourselves receive from God.*

I can remember every little detail about the day I lost my son, Riley. I had called the hospital the night before he was born because I was concerned that he wasn't moving. The nurse I spoke to told me to go to bed and rest. That next morning, I called my obstetrician and was told to go to the hospital because "today was the day." When we got there, the nurse hooked me up to the monitors. What I remember most was the COMPLETE SILENCE – no amniotic fluid swishing, no baby moving, and no heartbeat. The nurse, trying to be kind, said, "He must be hiding in there." But I knew! I knew our precious son had passed away. It took about two hours for the doctor to get there to give us the news, and as he gently rubbed my foot, he said, "Sometimes these things just happen." And the doctor nodded as my husband said, "You mean, he's gone?"

I used to wonder if I'd ever make it through such a dark time. But here I am today! I've watched as God has used my pain to display His great glory – to use me to love on others, to pray with and for the hurting, to show grace, mercy, and compassion to those who need that same comfort. What a gift, something I would not be nearly as good at had I not experienced this loss myself!

Friends, if you, too, need comfort, He is there, and I am praying for you. Know that the Lord asked me to specifically pray for anyone reading this who is hurting. Feel the prayers, feel His love, and feel His peace!

# Scripture

*Blessed and greatly favored is the man whose strength is in you [God], in whose heart are the highways to Zion. Passing through the Valley of Weeping (Baca), they make it a place of springs*

**Psalm 84:5-6, AMP**

# Questions to ponder

How has God comforted you in times of trial or hurting?

How can you now comfort those who need it?

Ask God if there is someone, in particular, you can come alongside to comfort.

# Journal

....................................................................

....................................................................

....................................................................

....................................................................

....................................................................

....................................................................

....................................................................

....................................................................

....................................................................

....................................................................

....................................................................

....................................................................

....................................................................

....................................................................

....................................................................

# 30 Rooted in Love

*Written by Alison Carson (my precious friend)*

Hello, SONShine!

There was a time in my life when I struggled with the concept of love. Not because I had a bad upbringing, but because there was a gaping hole in my life caused by a root of rejection. And the thing about any root is that it attracts fruit of the same nature, causing the root to grow deeper and stronger. In my case, it meant that I attracted rejection wherever I went. Ultimately, it led to self-hatred and suicidal thoughts.

At age seventeen, I became a Christian, and a dear mentor showed me this scripture: *And I pray that you, being rooted and established in love, may have power, together with all the Lord's holy people, to grasp how wide and long and high and deep is the love of Christ, and to know this love that surpasses knowledge – that you may be filled to the measure of all the fullness of God* (Ephesians 3:18-19).

Isn't it interesting that Paul prayed for us to be rooted in Jesus' love? No other root is meant to be part of our lives, for anything other than His love controls and destroys. By looking back at the way God created the world, we see that His original intent was for us to live in His love; it was human sin that removed us from this perfection. Thank God that, in His love, He made a way for us to return to Him and to abide in His love forever.

It took a loooong time for me to grasp the extent of Jesus' love – I had to seriously renew my mind! It's a journey, so these things are not immediate – the important thing is to start somewhere. But now, over twenty years later, I can say that the chains of rejection that held me bound have been broken ... and the root removed! I'm not perfect, but I know a Savior who is!

# Scripture

*For I am convinced that neither death nor life, neither angels nor demons, neither the present nor the future, nor any powers, neither height nor depth, nor anything else in all creation, will be able to separate us from the love of God that is in Christ Jesus our Lord*

**Romans 8:38-39**

# Questions to ponder

Is there a 'root' in your life that needs to be destroyed?

Ask God to reveal it to you and to shine the light of His truth into your heart. Meditate on and confess scriptures that speak specifically to your situation.

# Journal

........................................................................

........................................................................

........................................................................

........................................................................

........................................................................

........................................................................

........................................................................

........................................................................

........................................................................

........................................................................

........................................................................

........................................................................

........................................................................

........................................................................

........................................................................

# 31 Beauty for Ashes

Hello, SONshine!

I remember a time when a dear friend of mine was in a situation that she could not control. It was unfair and made no sense. See, she had been falsely accused of stealing several thousand dollars from her place of work. Overcome with anxiety and fear, she had no choice but to walk directly through it, laying it all at the cross, not knowing the outcome.

Sometimes, I wonder which is more difficult – experiencing tough times or watching someone else go through them. It hurts to watch people I care about go through difficulties. I imagine Jesus feels the same – He knows and feels our pain (see John 11:33-35).

During this particular time, I opened my Bible while praying, and Jesus brought me to Isaiah 61:3: *to bestow on them a crown of beauty instead of ashes, the oil of joy instead of mourning, and a garment of praise instead of a spirit of despair. They will be called oaks of righteousness, a planting of the Lord for the display of his splendor.*

What a wonderful promise! Yes, life can be harsh. It can be painful. It can leave deep wounds that penetrate the depths of our soul. Friends, we have all been in places of despair, of shattered dreams and suffering. Perhaps, for you, it is not the same as what my friend went through – maybe you've received a scary medical diagnosis, or you've been abused, mistreated, or abandoned. Or maybe you have been betrayed by a loved one. Whatever the situation, God knows, He intimately understands, and He will bring you through it, just like He did for my sweet friend.

## Scripture

*"I have told you these things, so that in me you may have peace. In this world you will have trouble. But take heart! I have over-come the world"*

**John 16:33**

## Questions to ponder

How have you seen God's glory displayed through your pain?

If you are in the midst of pain right now, how can you focus on God's strength to get you through?

# Journal

........................................................
........................................................
........................................................
........................................................
........................................................
........................................................
........................................................
........................................................
........................................................
........................................................
........................................................
........................................................
........................................................
........................................................
........................................................
........................................................

# 32 Cast the First Stone

Hello, SONshine!

A while ago, I read a Facebook post that said something like this: "The only person qualified to throw a stone ... chose not to."

I turned to John 8:1-11 and re-read the story that quote was referring to. It's about an adulterous woman who was brought before Jesus while He was teaching the people at the temple. Trying to trap Him so that they could accuse Him, the teachers of the law and the Pharisees asked, "In the Law Moses commanded us to stone such women. Now what do you say?" Jesus did not answer but knelt down and started writing on the ground. Relentless, His questioners continued until He stood up and responded, *"Let anyone of you who is without sin be the first to throw a stone at her."*

I can imagine what the scene must have looked like: Angry people, each holding a large stone in one hand, ready to kill this woman for her sin; the woman terrified of her pending death by stoning.

Whenever I read about this woman, I see all of us – sinners, saved by God's grace and given new life. Sometimes, I get so emotional thinking about how blessed we are that I am brought to tears with gratitude.

Though the woman deserved judgment, she received mercy. Instead of condemning her, Jesus instructed her to leave her sin behind – and I wouldn't be surprised if she became a follower of Jesus after that!

# Scriptures

---

*"Then neither do I condemn you,"* Jesus declared. *"Go now and leave your life of sin"*

**John: 8-11**

*Therefore, there is now no condemnation for those who are in Christ Jesus*

**Romans 8:1**

# Questions to ponder

---

What stones do you need to drop from your hand in order to show mercy to others?

Is there any sin in your life that you need to walk away from?

The Lord is here to help you. I promise!

# Journal

....................................................................
....................................................................
....................................................................
....................................................................
....................................................................
....................................................................
....................................................................
....................................................................
....................................................................
....................................................................
....................................................................
....................................................................
....................................................................
....................................................................
....................................................................

# 33 Death Was Conquered

Hello, SONshine!

Resurrection Sunday (Easter, as many call it) is one of the holidays that touches me the most. I just love this explanation that I found online: *"The word Easter is related to the word east, which naturally points us to the sunrise, to new days and new beginnings."*

To Christians, Easter is about a dead man who came back to life again. The Son of God Himself died and rose again to pay the price for our sins and reconcile us to God (Romans 4:25; 2 Corinthians 5:19). What this really means is that death was conquered – our sins are forgiven, and we are promised an eternity with the Lord. Whenever I think of Jesus' great sacrifice and His glorious resurrection, I am so grateful.

God is the One who raised Jesus from the dead, and amazingly, that 'resurrection power' now LIVES in all believers. His power within us can do anything in our lives (Ephesians 1:18-21). The meaning of this is that God can move mountains, split seas, restore lives, and roll away any stone – in our own lives, and through us into the lives of others. We can proclaim good news to the poor, freedom for the prisoners (prisoners of anything – addiction, greed, pride), and sight for the blind.

Ultimately, Jesus' resurrection means that LOVE is stronger than death. Love is why God gave His only Son (John 3:16), and love is why our risen Lord intercedes for His children (Romans 8:34).

The resurrection is hope – hope for everyone. It is new life, new beginnings, new birth!

# Scripture

*I ask – ask the God of our Master, Jesus Christ, the God of glory – to make you intelligent and discerning in knowing him personally, your eyes focused and clear, so that you can see exactly what it is he is calling you to do, grasp the immensity of this glorious way of life he has for his followers, oh, the utter extravagance of his work in us who trust him – endless energy, boundless strength!*

**Ephesians 1:17-19, MSG**

# Questions to ponder

How does this change the way you view God and His mighty power?

# Journal

...........................................................................................
...........................................................................................
...........................................................................................
...........................................................................................
...........................................................................................
...........................................................................................
...........................................................................................
...........................................................................................
...........................................................................................
...........................................................................................
...........................................................................................
...........................................................................................
...........................................................................................
...........................................................................................
...........................................................................................

# 34 Split the Sea

Hello, SONshine!

While getting ready for work one day, I heard the song "Split the Sea" by Hannah Kerr. We've probably all heard the story of God parting the Red Sea, one of the most spectacular miracles in the Bible.

The story is about the Israelites escaping slavery under the rule of Pharaoh. After Pharaoh agreed to let them go, he changed his mind (knowing that he was losing his free slave labor) and sent his army after them.

When the Israelites saw the Egyptian army chasing them, they were terrified and began to question why Moses had brought them out into the desert to die. After all, they would rather live in slavery than die in the desert.

Moses simply responded like this: *"Do not be afraid. Stand firm and you will see the deliverance the Lord will bring you today. The Egyptians you see today you will NEVER see again. The Lord will fight for you; you need only to be still"* (Exodus 14:13-14).

FRIENDS, this God – the God of Moses – is the SAME God we serve today. Whatever you are facing, we serve a God who has absolute power over ALL things. And He CAN still split the sea.

# Scriptures

Moses stretched out his hand over the sea, and all that night the LORD drove the sea back with a strong east wind and turned it into dry land. The waters were divided, and the Israelites went through the sea on dry ground, with a wall of water on their right and on their left

**Exodus 14:21-22**

Great is our Lord and mighty in power; his understanding has no limit

**Psalm 147:5**

# Questions to ponder

How has God made a way for you when it was seemingly impossible?

How is God fighting for you right now?

# Journal

.....................................................................................
.....................................................................................
.....................................................................................
.....................................................................................
.....................................................................................
.....................................................................................
.....................................................................................
.....................................................................................
.....................................................................................
.....................................................................................
.....................................................................................
.....................................................................................
.....................................................................................
.....................................................................................
.....................................................................................

# 35 Kindness

Hello, *SONshine!*

My community has a social media page called 'I'll Help' where people can request assistance with things they need. Often, when I look at the page and want to help, many others have already offered! It's easy to think of all the negatives that bombard us, but really, when we look around, we see so many people who show kindness. There are many people throughout the Bible who showed this characteristic as well (e.g., King David in 2 Samuel 9:1).

Being kind can have such an impact on those around us. I recall a time when God put a specific friend on my heart one morning. I sent her a text message to let her know that I was thinking of her and praying for her. Within seconds, I received a text message back saying how much my message meant to her. She told me that she had "been crying all morning" because it was the one-year anniversary of her mom's death. I hadn't known that, but God knew! He was just looking for a willing vessel to show kindness. I'm so glad I reached out to her that day (and didn't procrastinate until the next day or the next week!) because it taught me a powerful lesson that little acts of kindness can make the biggest difference.

Galatians 5:22 includes kindness as one of the fruits of the Spirit ('fruit' means something that comes as a result of living in the Spirit). Jesus so perfectly modeled all of the fruits of the Spirit, and as we continue to be transformed in our Christian lives, we spontaneously produce these fruits too. Kindness always comes from a gracious and gentle heart, from someone who has compassion and cares about others.

Whatever today brings, choose to be kind. Love you!

# Scripture

---

*But the Holy Spirit produces this kind of fruit in our lives: love, joy, peace, patience, kindness, goodness, faithfulness, gentleness, and self-control. There is no law against these things!*

**Galatians 5:22-23, NLT**

# Questions to ponder

---

Who in your life displays kindness?

What is one way you can show kindness today?

# Journal

..............................................................

..............................................................

..............................................................

..............................................................

..............................................................

..............................................................

..............................................................

..............................................................

..............................................................

..............................................................

..............................................................

..............................................................

..............................................................

..............................................................

..............................................................

# 36 The Unequipped

Hello, SONshine!

I've often thought about one of the most beloved women of all time – Jesus' mother, Mary. Can you imagine what must have gone through her mind when the angel of the Lord appeared to her and said, *"Greetings, you who are highly favored! The Lord is with you"* (Luke 1:28)? And how she must have felt when the angel said, *"Do not be afraid, Mary; you have found favor with God"* (Luke 1:30)? I imagine she was excited to hear the news that she was going to be a mother. Perhaps she started daydreaming about what it would be like to carry a child and what her special son would look like. And most likely, she probably questioned, "Why me?"

See, Mary was not chosen because of anything she owned, nor because of any skills or beauty she may have possessed. By all accounts, she was a young, poor girl, which, in that day, would have actually disqualified her for such a task. So, why was Mary chosen? Because she was totally and completely surrendered to God's will for her life.

If you ever feel that your own ability, education, or skills are inadequate, think of Mary. God does not call the equipped, He equips the called! Remember that. He has a very specific purpose for your life, so don't limit His choices by questioning your abilities. He can and will use you if you trust Him.

# Scriptures

---

*Trust in the Lord with all your heart and
lean not on your own understanding; in all
your ways submit to him, and he will make
your paths straight*

**Proverbs 3:5-6**

*For we live by faith, not by sight*

**2 Corinthians 5:7**

# Questions to ponder

---

What has God placed on your heart today?

Is there something He is calling you to do
that requires total surrender?

I am praying for you!

# Journal

........................................................
........................................................
........................................................
........................................................
........................................................
........................................................
........................................................
........................................................
........................................................
........................................................
........................................................
........................................................
........................................................
........................................................
........................................................

# 37 Coffee with a Friend

Hello, SONshine!

I've been thinking a lot about how we can make a difference for God's kingdom. Sometimes, I feel like such a small fish in a BIG ocean. How can I possibly influence enough people for Christ so that they too have salvation? One person comes to mind: A man who went to the same high school as me. Though we lost touch over the years, he recently reached out to several 'old' classmates through social media.

He, like so many, doesn't really know IF God exists. In fact, he is questioning more than ever now because he is dying of cancer and has been told he has a very short time left. Seeds have been planted, and a couple of people have even been very bold in trying to convince him that Jesus is real.

Yet, he is still unsure.

My sister and I were talking about his situation and praying for him when we were both brought to a verse in Isaiah that tells us specifically that sharing the gospel will always prosper. We may not always see the fruit of our actions, but we do know that seeds are planted.

God is speaking, and He will transform our hearts so that we can carry out HIS work.

Friend, doesn't this bring you peace? God is in control, and rest assured, God's Word will never, ever return empty. Love you.

# Scripture

*"The rain and snow come down from the heavens and stay on the ground to water the earth. They cause the grain to grow, producing seed for the farmer and bread for the hungry. It is the same with my word. I sent it out, and it always produces fruit. It will accomplish all I want it to, and it will prosper everywhere I send it"*

**Isaiah 55:10-11, NLT**

# Question to ponder

Have you ever shared your faith with someone who appeared uninterested in your message?

Be assured that you have planted seeds that God can water. Don't give up on sharing the good news of Jesus – it is always worth it.

# Journal

........................................................

........................................................

........................................................

........................................................

........................................................

........................................................

........................................................

........................................................

........................................................

........................................................

........................................................

........................................................

........................................................

........................................................

# 38 In the Fire

Hello, *SONshine!*

While listening to a Christian radio station, I heard a song with the lyrics, *"There was another in the fire standing next to me."* It refers to Shadrach, Meshach, and Abednego, the three Jews who refused to bow down to King Nebuchadnezzar's god (a golden statue he had made and to which he decreed that all should bow down and worship).

When the king heard of their refusal, he was full of rage and ordered them to be thrown into a blazing furnace (the punishment he had issued for all who disobeyed his command). He was so angry that he ordered the furnace to be turned up seven times hotter than normal, so much so that the flames killed the soldiers who took Shadrach, Meshach, and Abednego to the furnace.

But what of the three Jewish men? When the king looked into the blaze, he saw FOUR men walking around unharmed. Amazed, King Nebuchadnezzar summoned them out of the fire, and out they came, without even a hair on their heads burned, and with no smell of smoke.

See, the Lord was in the fire with them, protecting them, walking with them, and keeping them safe from harm.

Friends, no matter what you are facing, remember, there is another in the fire, and He is standing next to you.

## Scripture

*He said, "Look! I see four men walking around in the fire, unbound and unharmed, and the fourth looks like the son of the gods"*

**Daniel 3:25**

## Question to ponder

Are you in the midst of your own personal fire in which you see no way out?

God sees you; He hears you; He is standing there with you. You are not invisible.

# Journal

.............................................................
.............................................................
.............................................................
.............................................................
.............................................................
.............................................................
.............................................................
.............................................................
.............................................................
.............................................................
.............................................................
.............................................................
.............................................................
.............................................................
.............................................................

# 39 Quiet Seasons

Hello, SONshine!

Has there ever been a time in your life when you felt like God wasn't there? I call these 'quiet seasons' – times when it doesn't seem to matter how much you pray or read the Bible, you just can't feel God's presence.

Quiet seasons remind me of Job. Job was a wealthy and upright man, a man of God. He had a large family, many servants, and thousands of sheep, camels, and other livestock.

Satan came before God stating that Job was only faithful to Him because of his prosperity. So, God allowed Satan to completely destroy Job's life. Job lost all of his children, his servants, and his animals in one day! In addition to these great losses, God allowed Satan to cause Job physical suffering by covering him with painful sores.

I have to wonder, in the midst of this situation, whether Job wondered if God had deserted him. His wife and three close friends questioned God; his friends went so far as to say that Job must have committed terrible sins for the Lord to have allowed all the disasters to happen (many people still believe this big, fat lie of Satan's).

Despite this, Job did not lose his faith in God. He did, however, express his frustration and overwhelming grief, which shows us it's OK to be human, to have emotions, and to grieve. See, even though Job could not sense God's presence nor understand why those things happened, he knew that God was faithful and could be trusted. Job realized that when NOTHING else was left, he still had God, and that was enough.

Finally, God spoke through a mighty storm. Job fell in humble reverence, and God restored his fortunes, giving him twice as much as he had before.

Friends, I am sure, at times, we have all wondered whether God was present. And if that's you right now, the only advice I can give you is to simply trust. Sometimes, I pray, "I need You, Lord, front and center to intercede for me and to help me trust."

Love you!

## Scripture

*When Job prayed for his friends, the Lord restored his fortunes. In fact, the Lord gave him twice as much as before!*

**Job 42:10, NLT**

## Questions to ponder

In your life, when have you wondered if God was actually there?

Are you in a time like that right now?

In what way can you trust that He will carry you through it?

# Journal

...........................................................................
...........................................................................
...........................................................................
...........................................................................
...........................................................................
...........................................................................
...........................................................................
...........................................................................
...........................................................................
...........................................................................
...........................................................................
...........................................................................
...........................................................................
...........................................................................
...........................................................................

# 40 Royal Position

Hello, *SONshine!*

Each of our lives is a beautiful tapestry, pieced together very delicately and very intentionally by our Creator. This last devotion is about one of the most beautiful women in the Bible: Esther. Not only was she physically beautiful, but she also had immense inner beauty.

Esther was an orphaned Jew who was raised by Mordecai, her cousin. Through a series of events, Esther won the favor of the Persian king and was eventually crowned Queen. At Mordecai's request, she did not tell anyone she was a Jew.

Later, the king gave a man named Haman great honor by elevating him above all the other nobles. At the king's command, *all the royal officials at the king's gate knelt down and paid honor to Haman* – everyone that is, except Mordecai. This enraged Haman so much that he made a plot to have all the Jews killed (Esther 3:1-5).

Mordecai knew that only Esther could approach the king and expose this plan of genocide. But it was against the law to approach the king uninvited, and if you did not find favor, you would be killed. Naturally, Esther was afraid. Mordecai pointed Esther to a much higher purpose, saying, *"For if you remain silent at this time, relief and deliverance for the Jews will arise from another place, but you and your father's family will perish. And who knows but that you have come to your royal position for such a time as this?"* (Esther 4:14). In complete faith, Esther approached the king, found favor, and as a result, the Jews were saved.

In reading the story of Queen Esther, we can see that she was most definitely on the throne for *"such a time as this"* – a time to deliver the Jews from death.

See, we serve a God who very eloquently puts all the puzzle pieces of our lives together so that we can display HIS great glory. No matter what you face, God has all the tools to bring you through it and give you victory. Just like Esther, you are positioned to make decisions that would honor and glorify God. YOU are not here by accident! God has placed you exactly where you are and invites you, with confidence, to join in His work! Take that step of faith!

Love you!

## Scripture

*"And who knows but that you have come to your royal position for such a time as this?"*

**Esther 4:14**

## Questions to ponder

Where can you see God's hand at work in your life?

Is there something God is nudging you to do?

How can you come to your royal position "for such a time as this"?

# Journal

..........................................................

..........................................................

..........................................................

..........................................................

..........................................................

..........................................................

..........................................................

..........................................................

..........................................................

..........................................................

..........................................................

..........................................................

..........................................................

..........................................................

..........................................................

..........................................................

# Ready to Meet Jesus

Our SONshine family is so happy that you have chosen to give your life to the Lord. Following the Lord is the most important decision you will ever make; and God makes it very simple for us.. Romans 10:9 makes this promise: If you declare with your mouth, "Jesus is Lord," and believe in your heart that God raised him from the dead, you will be saved.

This is an example of a prayer you can pray to ask Jesus to dwell in your heart, or you can say your own prayer:

*"Dear Lord Jesus, I believe that You died on the cross for my sins, and I believe in my heart that God raised You from the dead. I accept You as my Lord and Savior, and I give You my life. I accept Your free gift of grace and salvation. Thank You for forgiving me, saving me, and giving me this gift of an eternity spent with You!"*

You, my sweet sister, are now saved. Welcome to the family! Congratulations! I join with all the angels in celebrating your new life in Christ Jesus.

*"In the same way, I tell you, there is rejoicing in the presence of the angels of God over one sinner who repents"* (Luke 15:10).

# References

**A Grateful Heart**
Gaither, G. L. and Gaither, W. J. (2015) *Jesus, I Heard You Had a Big House.* Gaither Vocal Group.
From the album: I Am A Promise (singing their favorite Gaither children's songs)

**You Are Not Alone**
Hall, J. M., Herms, B., and Nordeman, N. E. (2016) *Oh My Soul.* Casting Crowns.
From the album: The Very Next Thing

**A Masterpiece**
Warren, J. (2012) *The Purpose Driven Life: What on Earth Am I Here For?* Michigan. Zondervan. p.76.

**My Best Friend**
*https://en.wikipedia.org/wiki/Friendship#cite_note-1*
[accessed June 2020]

**Death was Conquered**
*https://www.gotquestions.org/meaning-of-Easter.html*
[accessed June 2020]

## In the Fire

Davenport, C. and Houston, T. (2019) *Another In The Fire*. Australia: Hillsong Music and Capitol Christian Music Group.

From the album: People

CPSIA information can be obtained
at www.ICGtesting.com
Printed in the USA
JSHW030650220722
28293JS00001B/5